WHERE
HAS MY
CEILING GONE?

IS THIS IT?
IS THIS AS GOOD AS MY LIFE GETS?

Warren Veenman & Sally Eichhorst

Reach Publishers
Self-publishers and Distributors of all books

...inspire the world
with words.

First published in 2002 by Reach Publishers

ISBN 9780620297240

Published by Reach Publishers, P.O.Box, 1384, Wandsbeck, South Africa, 3631
Printed and bound by Pinetown Printers (Pty) Ltd, 16 Ivy Road, Pinetown, 3600
Edited by Janine Williams for Reach Publishers
Cover designed by Reach Publishers

Website: www.aimtoinspire.com

E-mail: reach @webstorm.co.za

By Warren Veenman & Sally Eichhorst
Unleash Your Full Potential
Dare To Succeed
A Pocket Full of Inspiration
A Burst of Inspiration
I Can't...

By Sally Eichhorst
If I Can You Can
Get Your Act Together

A mouse awoke with a big fright,
for his ceiling had disappeared overnight.
"Where's my ceiling gone?" he lamented.
"Why not move? I'm sure you could even find a better place,"
his friend commented.
"Do you really think I could do better?" Squealed the mouse,
surveying his roofless house.
"Look around you mate
and ask yourself, is this it? Is this my fate?"
"Well, I never really had to think about it before. I guess, I just
accepted that this is as good as it gets and never really noticed
what my life lacks.
"But now I wonder, is there more out there for me – a better
home, a higher ceiling, a new life perhaps?"
The little mouse now became quite excited.
What had begun as a disaster, he now invited.
Indeed, he moved to a better home
and keeps improving on it, like an enlightened King upon his
throne.
He learnt a valuable lesson that day,
which he repeats to all those he finds along his way.
"You create your own ceiling in Life! Learn to lift your ceiling
to see further, more clearly and give yourself room to grow.
"I am telling you this because I know."

Sally Eichhorst

Contents

#

B y reading this book you are going to embark on an amazing journey that can change every aspect of your life for the better. It is like no other motivational book you have or will ever read.

We all want to improve our lives in some way. Unfortunately, for most of us this remains only a dream, never to become a reality! The most important reason why we don't achieve the life we want, is quite simply because we do not believe that we can. Whether we want to make more money, start our own business, write a novel, change our job, discover the world, or just find a companion, we don't bother pursuing these goals because we think that they are out of our reach. This belief is due to a combination of influences surrounding us, which unconsciously cause us to create in our mind an "invisible ceiling." This ceiling stops us from seeing what we are capable of by limiting our belief in ourselves.

Imagine the vast possibilities we could visualize and the

amazing things we could do, if we were somehow able to raise this "self-made, invisible ceiling?" The good news is that because this "invisible ceiling" in your mind is self-created, you can learn to raise it no matter what your present circumstances.

This book aims to show you how to raise your ceiling in life so that there are no barriers to hold you back from achieving the life of your dreams.

This inspirational book follows the remarkable fable of a man who was able to raise his ceiling far beyond what was deemed possible. The following pages cover his personal struggle to discover the secrets to success and during his journey, nine life-skills are highlighted, the lessons which ultimately take him from rags to riches!

The story is based on fact and you will discover that you can often identify with the characters. Indeed, somewhere during this journey, you should find yourself and learn how to raise your ceiling and achieve far beyond your expectations. This book will move you emotionally, uplift you mentally and drive you forward on the road toward your perfect life.

We invite you to become one with this character, stepping into his shoes and walking with him along his journey of discovery. See the world through his eyes and most of all learn from the vitally important life skills along the way.

Read on and see how one man discovered the secrets of success – secrets that will become yours to do as you please with.

"Is this it?
Is this as good as my life will ever get?"
No! I don't think so, there's more I'll bet.

There's always more
for those who are willing to see beyond their
ceiling and door.

Raise your ceiling or remove it altogether and
you will see
that your life can be everything you ever
dreamed it should be.

Part 1
Limiting Beliefs

Nothing can stop a person from succeeding, when they have a strong belief in themselves. Nothing can help a person from failing, when they have no belief in themselves.

Sally & Warren

Chapter 1
A Crushing Ceiling

I am going to tell you a story that I believe will change your life. Who am I? I am a legendary storyteller among my people. For years, this has been our way to pass on our culture and traditions. I have many stories to share, passed from generation to generation, but this story must be told to as many people who will listen. A good story is one that has the ability to change your life for the better. This is one of those stories. Tell it to all you meet, in particular to your children and to their children. Let it be shared, learned, remembered and most importantly acted upon by all you know.

This is the fable of twin brothers who were born into a poor and humble family. Home was a tiny doorless shack thrown together with cardboard, wood and corrugated iron. An old, black plastic sheet hung in tatters from the doorway offering a little privacy. Similar shacks were scattered in all directions as far as the eye could see. It was so jam-packed that it was often difficult to find walking space between the shanty dwellings.

There was no electricity or running water in the settlement. Toilets were simply holes in the ground, situated on the outskirts and shared by thousands of dwellers. Seldom was there not a long line of people waiting to take their turn and sometimes if the wind was strong and blew in the wrong direction, the stench from the toilets would hang over the settlement like a foul cloud for days.

The arrival of the twins was greeted with just a hint of superstition by their parents and fellow shack dwellers. You see, these were simple people, who still believed in much of the old superstitions, which included the idea of twins as an unnatural and suspicious occurrence.

One twin was named John, but soon earned the nickname Chuck, short for chuckle, due to his jovial nature. As a baby he never stopped smiling and with time his beaming smile and loud laughter made him a popular young boy to all that knew him. His twin brother was named Michael and later nicknamed Chip because he was so much like his father - a "chip" off the old block. From infancy he looked very much like his father and this resemblance grew stronger and all the more evident in his character as the boy grew older.

The twins' schooling was limited. At the age of 14, as soon as they had completed their Std. 6 at a rundown local school, their father had insisted that it was time for the boys to help him earn a living. Chuck had been disappointed as he enjoyed studying and had hoped to one day become a teacher. But he had understood that his parents could no longer afford to educate them and needed their help to survive.

So the twins had sacrificed their education to help their father scratch out a living. Every day they would wake up at the crack of dawn and make their way down to the local rubbish dumps. There they would all sift through the garbage in the hope of finding reusable items for resale to people from the settlement and to second hand stores.

Wednesdays were the most exciting days. Every Wednesday they would wander much further afield into what they considered to be "the rich area" and sift through their rubbish. This was always a good day as they always found plenty of useful things. They were often amazed at the wonderful things these people simply threw away or wasted.

On these days the twins loved to look into the yards of the "rich people." They would stare at the beautiful houses and admire the nice cars parked in the driveways, envying the people who lived there.

They often wondered, like so many other youngsters in the settlement, if this was it? Was this as good as their life would ever get? Indeed they believed it to be so. Their parents had told them this hundreds of times and so they believed it, just like their parents and their parents before them. This was the limit to how far they could go in life. Even their neighbours and friends often explained that you were either lucky and born into the good things in life, or you were born into poverty, with no opportunities. They said one simply had to accept one's lot in life and that was that. Unknowingly, they had all created their own low and stifling ceiling in life so that they could not see any opportunities to better their situation.

So the twins were forced to accept that this was their life. Although they plodded on from day to day, they never stopped envying those from the "rich area", who had homes of brick and cement, hot water, electricity, a car and nice clothes. Chuck had received the wrath of his father once when he had told him about his dream of becoming a teacher and having the good things in life. His father had become enraged telling Chuck to stop dreaming about silly things that could never be. He said that they were all lucky to even have food on the table and a roof over their heads.

From that day on, the matter was closed. Chuck kept his dreams and deepest feelings hidden and soon the invisible ceiling to his potential became even lower, almost crushing his dreams altogether so that he believed that achieving them was indeed impossible.

Then one day everything changed for Chuck. It happened on a Wednesday, while rummaging through the rubbish of one of the "rich people." He'd found a crumpled book and on opening it was at once mesmerized by the words inside. It was full of motivational quotes and poems, which seemed to reach out and speak to him on a very personal level. At night, lying atop his grass mat on the floor of the shack, he would wait until he was sure everyone was asleep. Then he would light a candle and read his treasured book, studying each poem and quote carefully and reading them over and over again. He even kept his favourite poem in his pocket and found a plastic sleeve to protect it for it was the most prized possession he had. This poem he read again and again until its words were carved into his mind forever.

> *If you think you are beaten, you are;*
> *If you think you dare not; you don't;*
> *If you'd like to win, but think you can't;*
> *It's almost a cinch you won't.*
>
> *If you think you'll lose, you're lost;*
> *For out in the world we find*
> *Success begins with a fellow's will,*
> *It's all in the state of mind.*
> *Life's battles don't always go*
> *To the stronger or faster man;*
> *But soon or late the man who wins*
> *Is the one who thinks he can.*

Anonymous

Chuck had a special place where he often went to be alone and think. It was high on top of a hill overlooking the "big city". Far in the distance he could also see the beautiful brick houses of the wealthy area. A busy freeway ran directly below and he would watch the cars speeding in both directions to a life that he wished he had.

He would sit on the hill and think about the things he'd read in the crumpled book he'd found. Looking at everything before him, he simply could not accept that all those people out there with cars, houses, well-paying jobs and happy families had been lucky. In fact, he even knew of some people who had been brought up in these shacks and had left to make a better life for themselves. If they could, then surely he could too?

He thought constantly about these things and he slowly started to realize that this can't be it. This was not as good as it gets for him. There had to be a better life out there. This desire to better himself and his situation became a strong belief within him. Without realizing it, Chuck was raising his ceiling by believing that he had the potential to make more of his life.

He had discovered the first of nine important life skills. Listen carefully now to the first lesson, for it was the beginning of a great journey of discovery towards success for Chuck. Take heed, for it may also be the beginning for you.

Life Skill 1
Raise Your Ceiling

The first skill each and every one of us should learn, if we are to have any chance of bettering our lives and reaching our dreams, is to develop a strong positive belief in ourselves and our capabilities.

The beliefs we have about ourselves are responsible for who we ultimately become and what we eventually achieve in life. Indeed, a positive self-belief is a prerequisite for achieving anything and everything in life.

If you believe that you will fail, you will! If you believe that you will succeed, you will! If you believe you will be rich, you will be rich. If you believe you are destined for poverty, you will never rise above that. It is a fact, that you become like the person you think and believe you are and achieve only what you think and believe you are capable of.

Right from the start, Chuck had to learn this first life skill. He had to believe that he had the capability of making a better life for himself and that he deserved this life before he could even begin to move forward and go after it. Before we can even begin to imagine what it is we want from life, we first have to believe that we have the capability to achieve great possibilities. Without this belief, we would never even attempt to do anything about our dreams. What's the point of imagining a better life when we have already convinced ourselves that we are incapable of achieving it?

Don't be fooled into believing that "you've either got it or you haven't and there is nothing you can do about it." This is one of the most common misconceptions and is why people do not rise above their situation.

If you do not believe me, I want you to think about those who have yet to be born. They will eventually grab at the very opportunities you missed, rising to the top of their professions, running their own successful companies and enjoying great wealth. Amongst them, will also be those who are going to become the great leaders of tomorrow, Presidents of their nations and athletic stars. I believe that you have an advantage over them as you are alive now and they have yet to be born.

It's easy to say "Believe in yourself and you will succeed," but how do you develop a powerful belief in yourself?

Just like Chuck did, you have to ask yourself, "What limiting beliefs do I have?" Then work on getting rid of them and rather focus on uplifting and positive beliefs.

Let's list some of Chuck's limiting beliefs:

- *You are either lucky enough to be born into the good life or destined for poverty.*

- *He should forget about becoming a teacher as he has no education.*
- *He should be satisfied with what he has and stop wishing for more.*

Chuck began to rid himself of these limiting beliefs by refusing to accept them. He began to convince himself, that he was destined for better things and could rise above his situation to achieve his dreams.

There is a popular saying that goes, "You create your own ceiling in life!" What it means, is that you unconsciously set your own limits to what you can and cannot do, due to your beliefs about yourself and your capabilities. The more limiting beliefs you have about yourself, the lower your self-created ceiling will be and the less you will achieve. When you start to rid yourself of limiting beliefs, you raise your ceiling and are able to achieve more. In this way Chuck had unknowingly raised the ceiling to his potential.

I have met many successful people in my time. All of them had one very important thing in common – before they succeeded in any way, they first believed they could. They valued themselves highly, choosing to raise their ceiling and refusing to accept any limitations to their potential.

You must learn to believe in yourself and your capabilities. Your beliefs hold great power. They make up the person you become and will influence what you achieve in life. I want you to start believing that you can do anything you truly put your mind to. If you believe you can, you will go to great lengths to prove yourself right. However, if you believe you can't, you will make no effort and you will fail as your ceiling will be so low that you will see no opportunities to better your life at all.

Now I have shared with you the first vital life skill on the road to success. Note it well, for when you start believing you can, the ceiling to your potential will rise a little higher so you can see further and achieve a great deal more.

Let me now return to the twins ...

Part 2
Imagine The Possibilities

Every great achievement was once impossible.

Anon

Chapter 2

If You Can Dream It You Can Do It

Now I must tell you about the turning point in Chuck's young life. A time of great sadness for the twins, yet also a time of self-discovery and growth for Chuck.

It happened one night in July – the dry season, when rain was scarce and the Winter drought turned everything from luscious greens to crackling browns. During this time, fires were common and the people knew all too well about the devastation these hot spreading monsters left behind.

On that particular night, Chuck and Chip were filled with boyish excitement as they had arranged to meet with two young sisters living on the outskirts of the settlement. The boys had had their eyes on Thandi and Philile for some time and had at last worked up the courage to approach them. There was much girlish giggling and eye fluttering as the girls agreed to the meeting and Chuck thought his heart would explode when Thandi looked him in the eye and smiled shyly at him. She was surely the most beautiful creation he had ever laid his eyes on.

That evening, as the twins had walked for half an hour to reach the girls' home, they were both filled with the carefree wonder of love. Life seemed good for a while, as they forgot about who they were, where they came from and what they did not have. They'd never had much to be excited about in their young lives, but now there was the exciting promise of love to explore. For a time that evening, chatting to Thandi and Philile, holding hands and laughing heartily, the twins were happier than at any time they could remember.

It's a strange thing how our happiest moments can so quickly be followed by our saddest. It seemed terribly unfair to rob the young boys of their most memorable and happiest time only to replace the memory of that evening with one so painful.

Just before the twins were about to say good-bye to their young loves and while they were contemplating the serious matter of their first ever farewell kiss and hug, the news came to them. Fire! The news spread like the fire itself – very quickly.

A mostly sleepy-eyed community was rudely awakened by the smoke and crackling heat, which tore through the settlement, claiming many lives and homes as it spread. Fuelled by thatch, grass and wood, it was unstoppable, burning its way through hundreds of shacks before the people could even begin to get it under control.

Don't worry, Chuck and Chip were quite safe on the outskirts of the settlement for the fire was on the opposite side. But they ran like men possessed towards the smoldering remains of the fire, for it had come from the vicinity of their home. The path of destruction they had followed as they ran panic stricken into the night towards their shack had been like that of a war zone.

It is a very sad thing to lose everything at the tender age of seventeen years. A time when life as a young man should be beginning, is not a time for so many endings. Their home was gone along with everything in it. Their parents were missing along with countless others, all presumed dead.

Those poor boys sat for hours staring blankly at what had once been their home. They had waited, at first hopeful for their parents' return, both fighting the possibility of what they feared to be the truth. It was an evening the twins would never forget – one of great loss and sorrow. With the loss of their parents, overnight they had been forced to become men.

As the months had passed the twins had slowly come to grips with their loss and had become all the more dependant on one another. With the help of neighbours, along with odds and ends they had picked up during their foraging, they had managed to put together a small ramshackle home where their former shack had stood. It was nowhere near as spacious and sturdy as the original, but it was something. They continued to wake up early each morning to sift through the dumps as their father had taught them and for awhile it seemed like nothing had changed other than the obvious absence of their parents.

For Chuck however, much had changed. Even before this dramatic event in his life, he had been restless. Prior to the fire, he had already begun to believe that he could do better – that there was more to life than sifting through other peoples' castaways. He dared to believe in himself and his ability to rise above his situation and move on to greater things.

After the fire had taken everything from him, his dreams of a better life were at first shattered. But then he began to think – "I want more from my life. I know I can do better. I want to be a teacher."

These thoughts played around in his head and each day after the fire he became even more determined to search for a better life and make his dreams come true.

He had tried on numerous occasions to talk to Chip about his thoughts and dreams, but Chip's reaction had always been much like their father's had been. He would become angry, laughing mockingly at Chuck, telling him that he lived with his head in the clouds, dreaming of things that could never be. "You're a fool", he'd say. "It's time you come back down to earth and live in the real world where the poor get poorer and the rich get richer. How could you even imagine becoming a teacher? You will never be more than someone who sifts through other people's garbage – just accept it and be content!"

But Chuck could not shake off the restlessness he felt. He would lie awake at night thinking continuously of a better life. He started to yearn for it and it started to eat at him like a parasite demanding attention. It was a constant nagging within him to do more, be more and see more. Chuck began to visualize himself as a teacher, seeing the eager young faces smiling back at him. He could see himself behind the wheel of his car, driving into the garage of his nice brick home and happily greeting Thandi, his beautiful and pregnant wife at the door. Now that was the life he wanted!

The more Chuck visualized these dreams and desires, the clearer the picture became in his mind and the more restless and determined he became to make them a reality. He would sit for hours on the hill visualizing his ideal life until it became a burning desire within him to make it all happen. He believed he was destined for better things and now he had a clear idea of exactly what he wanted.

Chuck's story has now brought us to the second valuable life skill needed to achieve your dreams in life.

Life Skill 2
Know What You Want

I am an old man who has met many people. I have learnt a great deal from these people about success and failure. The most important thing I learnt, was that those who succeeded all had one thing in common, which was that they each had a clear picture in their minds of what they wanted from life. On the other hand those who failed or never achieved much had no idea of what they wanted.

So, listen carefully when I say that to improve upon your life and reach your dreams you must imagine exactly what you want. Think about it, how can you ever hope to achieve anything if you cannot even picture it to begin with? Knowing what you want is the first step to achieving it.

All the people I know who have achieved great things started with only a dream and did not question "how" or "if" they would achieve it. You must do the same! So I ask you to do what Chuck did and dream of all the things you want from life and to believe that you can achieve them. Forget "how" or "if"

- that comes later. If you keep thinking of "how" you will achieve it or "if" you can do it, you will limit yourself and will not achieve anything.

So, don't limit yourself. Allow yourself to imagine great and wonderful possibilities. All achievements started off as dreams. So can yours.

After all these years of watching and learning from people, it still amazes me how many of them have no idea of what they really want from life. Do you?

If you walk into a shop and do not know what you want, you will either walk out empty-handed or with something you don't really want or need. In the same respect, if you don't really know what you want from life, you will drift aimlessly, never quite getting anywhere. This is why it is vital that you have a clear and detailed idea of what you want from life.

When people tell me that they cannot imagine what they really want from life, I always ask them to do this simple task, which I now want you to do. Imagine that you are old like me and you are happily looking back over your life. What would you like to see? What would you like to have done with your life? Where would you have travelled? What would you have to show for all your years? Your answers to all these questions will be what you truly want from life. You must now start picturing these things again and again so that they become a clear idea in your mind of what you really want.

I have now shared with you the second vital life skill on the road to success. Again, I ask you to heed it well, for when you have a clear idea of what you want from life, you are already half way to achieving it.

You are probably eager to return to the story of the twins, so let me continue ...

Part 3
Mapping Out Your Dreams

If only we planned our lives as well as we plan for major events, for life is indeed the biggest event of all.

Warren & Sally

Chapter 3

What Is Stopping You?

As I mentioned before, Chuck was particularly fond of Wednesdays, as it was on Wednesdays that they would sift through the "rich peoples" rubbish. Inevitably he would always find something of value. That Wednesday he certainly found an item of great value, not only because of what it was and what it contained, but mostly because of the life-changing events that followed its discovery.

Chuck had found a very large, brown leather wallet. It was thick with wads of notes, credit cards, business cards, drivers' license and all sorts of slips and receipts usually found within an overstuffed wallet.

The large black rubbish bag in which he had found the wallet had been placed outside an enormous white Spanish style home. Without thinking twice, Chuck had buzzed at the gate.

A maid had answered and before giving him a chance to explain, she'd told him that there were no vacancies and that her boss did not wish to buy anything from him. Chuck had quickly interrupted her and had explained about the wallet. She'd asked him to wait and five minutes later she'd announced that her boss had indeed misplaced his wallet and was very grateful. She said that he wanted Chuck to come inside so that he could thank him personally.

The large gates had then opened and Chuck had nervously walked down the long, steep driveway towards the big white, double-storey house.

He'd approached the door hesitantly and before he'd even had a chance to knock, the door was flung open. He'd been greeted by a tall, well-built man in his late forties. A large, warm smile of welcome had stretched across the man's handsome face and Chuck could not help grinning sheepishly in response.

The man had introduced himself as Colby, the owner of the house. He worked from home and was dressed casually in a pair of shorts and T-shirt. He'd invited Chuck into his finely furnished, air conditioned office.

Chuck had quickly handed him the wallet and had watched as Colby opened it and made a quick inspection of the contents. He had then looked up and winked at Chuck, whistling and shaking his head in disbelief. Chuck was worried that he had found something amiss when in reality Colby was amazed that nothing had been taken – not even the cash – not one single note.

The man had then done something which took Chuck completely off-guard and which he'd never forget as long as he lived. He'd insisted that Chuck take all the money. He told Chuck he'd earned it through his honesty and goodness. He'd said that such a good heart and honesty deserved a reward.

It was more money than Chuck had ever had or seen at any one time in his life. Colby said he was just so grateful to have all his credit cards and license back. The money, he again insisted, Chuck had earned through his selfless act of returning the wallet.

Chuck had shyly accepted the thick pile of notes, tucking them deeply into the safety of his pants pocket. His hand had lingered there for a moment checking the pocket for holes – just in case.

Colby had seemed in no hurry to get rid of Chuck. He sat back in his chair and asked Chuck about himself. Where did he come from? What did he do? So Chuck had told Colby his short life history. "My dream is to one day become a teacher sharing my knowledge with others and helping them to better their lives," he'd finished off. He'd waited for the man to laugh in his face as everyone else had done, but the man did not. Instead he'd leaned forward in his chair gazing intently at Chuck and asked, "So what is stopping you from becoming a teacher?"

Again this man had taken Chuck off-guard. He had not expected such a question. There were many reasons why he could not become a teacher. He told Colby that he had so much against him. There were countless things stopping him from reaching this dream, that it just seemed impossible. In fact everyone else had told him it was impossible.

Colby had leaned back again grinning. "It's not impossible. Nothing is impossible, unless you think or make it so. In fact, in your case, I believe it's quite possible." He'd said to an astonished Chuck.

Astonishment turned to excitement as Colby had continued. "If I showed you the road that will lead you to your dreams – the road to anyone's dreams – would you follow it, no matter what?" Colby had asked.

Chuck had been unable to contain his enthusiasm as he'd blurted out excitedly – "Yes, just tell me what to do and I'll do it!"

Colby had then told Chuck that there were three things he needed to do before he could show him the road to his dreams.

The first thing was for Chuck to go back home and write down all the reasons that were stopping him from achieving his dream of becoming a teacher. "Now listen carefully", Colby had warned Chuck, "You must write down every single thing stopping you - no matter how big or small it is. Next, I want you to come back on Wednesday with your list and I will tell you the second thing you must do before I show you the road to achieving your dreams."

Chuck had told no one about finding the wallet, his meeting with Colby or the money he'd received. He hid the money away safely and as instructed, he went home and thought long and hard about his dream of becoming a teacher. Over the next few days, he had drawn up a long list of reasons that were stopping him from achieving this dream.

Some of them included:

- Lack of education
- No money
- Not knowing what to teach
- Not knowing how to get started
- Insecurity
- No family or peer support

The list had seemed endless, but eventually he felt that he had written down all possible reasons.

Chuck had been a little disheartened by this long list, but he was convinced that Colby would miraculously solve all these problems for him.

The following Wednesday, he was back at Colby's large Spanish style home and had eagerly handed Colby his long list. Chuck had been rather disappointed when Colby did not even glance at the list. Instead he'd given it back to Chuck, telling him that the second thing he had to do before he was shown the road to his dreams was to find a solution for each and every problem that he had written down.

Chuck could not believe what he was hearing. He had expected Colby to have an easy and clear-cut solution to all his problems. "I want you to go back home and next to each one of your reasons or problems, I want you to write down the solution." Colby had said. "Come back again next Wednesday and I promise you the road to your dreams will be revealed."

Chuck had left with a heavy heart. He had a sinking feeling that he would never be able to find solutions for all the obstacles on his list. It just seemed impossible, although Colby had insisted before he'd left that for every problem there is a solution and when you are geared towards finding solutions instead of focussing on problems, it's amazing how easily they come to you.

To Chuck's surprise and pleasure he found that Colby had indeed been right and the solutions were a lot easier to come up with than he had expected. It had taken him the entire week to write down a full description of every solution for each reason, but eventually he had completed the task and could barely wait for Wednesday.

Wednesday came and once more Chuck found himself inside Colby's home excitedly handing over his list of reasons and solutions.

Again Colby barely looked at the piece of paper Chuck had given to him. Instead he looked Chuck in the eye and asked earnestly, "If you complete all of these solutions, will you achieve your dream of becoming a teacher?"

"Of course!" Had been Chuck's immediate reply.

He'd then handed Chuck's list back to him saying, "Well Chuck, you are now holding the map that will show you how to reach your dream. Every one of those solutions on your list is like a sign that will direct you on the right road to your destination. If you had to organize these solutions in the right order, in other words, what you can do immediately should be on the top of your list, then this will become a distinct path leading you to your dream.

"So Chuck, you tell me now what the third and final step is?" Colby had asked.

"That's easy," Chuck said grinning at Colby. "I see now that all I have to do is rearrange my solutions in the correct sequence and they will lead me to my dream."

"You've got it!" Colby replied. "This is how you can make all your dreams come true. It's what I did and I'm living the life of my dreams. Whenever I want to achieve something, no matter how difficult or impossible it may seem at the time, I do the three things I have just explained to you."

They spoke for many hours enjoying one another's company for the last time. It was a sad farewell as Colby was leaving for New Zealand the following week and did not expect to return. The man from the big white house had taught him the next invaluable life skill to achieving your dreams in life.

Life Skill 3
Plan It!

*R*emember earlier, I asked you to think about what you really want from life and to forget about how to achieve it. Well, now we deal with the "How!"

As Chuck learnt from Colby, in order to know how to achieve anything you really want from life, the first thing you have to do is to list all the reasons or conditions that are preventing you from reaching this goal right now? You see, to achieve anything, you must know what is standing in your way so that you can deal with each problem effectively. If you know this, you are already halfway there.

Once you know each and every problem stopping you from reaching your dream, next to each of these setbacks, write down the solutions needed to overcome every one of them.

You will find like Chuck did, that these answers seem to flow effortlessly. I have also found from experience that there is a solution to almost any problem you may encounter, if you are willing to look at it from all angles.

Once you have listed all the solutions to the problems on your list, you must then organise these solutions effectively. Let me tell you how I have always done it. I start with a clear picture in my mind of what I want. I see my list of solutions like the pieces of a jigsaw puzzle. All the pieces are there, but they are all mixed up. I now have to organise them, piece by piece, in order to have the completed picture of what I want before me. In the same way, you have all the solutions to achieving your dream before you, but they are all muddled up. You must now organise them in the correct sequence in order to achieve the desired result.

The easiest way to organise your solutions in the proper sequence is to look at your end result (what you want to achieve) and work your way backwards one step at a time until you arrive at something you can do right now! By working your way backwards, you can design the pathway to attaining your dreams.

Always remember that your life is a journey and as with any journey, you will get lost without a map to guide you. Your plan is your map. With a well thought out and realistic plan, you will be amazed at what you can achieve.

I'm sure you have heard enough from an old man rambling on, so let me continue with the twins' story...

Part 4
Begin Somewhere

*Even if you are on the right track,
you'll get run over if you just sit there.*

Will Rogers

Chapter 4
Make Your Move!

An enthusiastic Chuck returned home after his last meeting with Colby full of ideas and positive energy. He was excited about finally having a plan to achieve his dream and could hardly wait to share the news with Chip.

Unfortunately Chip put an immediate damper on his enthusiasm, bursting Chuck's bubble as he sneered at the plan Chuck had eagerly shown him.

Chuck was hurt and disappointed although he should have expected such a reaction from his brother. Chip was almost vicious in his criticism of Chuck's plan. "How can you imagine that you could ever succeed at completing each solution. It's simply not possible! If you really believe that, then you're more of a fool than I thought," he'd screamed, tossing the neatly written plan Chuck had handed to him aside as though it was a piece of rubbish. "If you'd spend more time helping me instead of daydreaming, maybe we'd both be a lot better off. All that nonsense messes up your head and makes you dissatisfied with what you've got," he'd said.

Well, as so often happens in life, Chuck soon found himself back in his old routine. It wasn't so much a matter of giving up his dream. He still dreamed of becoming a teacher, but in the meantime life had to go on and soon the weeks turned into months and still Chuck had done nothing about his dream. Although he felt trapped in his life, it was the only one he knew.

Chuck knew with certainty that the longer he stayed where he was, the harder it would eventually be to leave. You see, he felt safe and secure where he was, as everything was familiar and routine. It was comforting to know that he had a roof over his head, no matter how pathetic it was. The knowledge that his brother and friends were nearby was also reassuring. The surrounding area and the way the people operated was familiar to him and sifting through garbage was the only thing he knew for sure that he could do. The thought of leaving this safe environment for the unknown was indeed frightening. Change is always uncomfortable and many of us look upon it with great hesitation. Chuck knew that to become too comfortable would put an end to his dreams of a better life, but still much time passed and nothing changed.

Then one hot summer night something changed within Chuck. He had been lying on his tattered and badly stained mattress, which he had been ecstatic to find shortly after the fire. He was staring up at their makeshift tin roof when he had noticed a crack in the ceiling almost directly above his head. His eyes had lingered on the crack for a moment before moving on to the starlit night beyond.

He'd been amazed by the brightness of the stars and the vast number of them that he could see through the small crack. Suddenly, he'd been overcome with the desire to see more. He'd almost wished that there was no ceiling over his head to limit his view of the night sky above. He'd imagined that he could see forever and for a moment he'd thought about being one of those stars and looking back down upon himself and the rest of the world. What would he see? He'd see a big, wonderful world, full of opportunities. He'd see himself trapped between four small walls of his dilapidated shack. A shack with a cracked ceiling that was far too low and stifling. Overall, he'd see a life that was unfulfilling and frustrating.

With startling clarity, Chuck had finally seen the stark reality of his situation as it truly was. He knew that there was a better life beyond those four walls and that cracked ceiling waiting for him to discover.

He remembered reading the following words from the tattered old motivational book he had found – "Remove your ceiling and the sky's the limit." All at once he'd understood what those words meant and imagined the vast potential that lay out there if he wanted it. Lying there that hot summer night, Chuck realized that the ceiling was really a limit – a lid on his potential. It represented everything that was keeping him from moving forward and growing in life. It followed that the first step to removing his ceiling would be to break away from the bonds that were holding him there and keeping him from seeking out the life he wanted.

Another very important fact had dawned on Chuck that night. Something quite simple really, although it is often the reason why so many people never achieve their dreams in life. It occurred to Chuck that it was wonderful for him to dream about having the good things in life and even to know how to get them, but they would remain only dreams and wishes unless he did something to make them a reality.

He then envisaged himself years later, an old and bitter man still lying on the same battered mattress and looking up through the same old crack in the ceiling, wondering what had happened to the years and to all his dreams. A shudder had run through him at the thought of this image and he was determined never to be that old man.

He then remembered Colby's last words to him as they had said their farewell at the door – "Let me give you just one last word of advice Chuck – start now doing something from your plan, no matter how small or you'll never start at all!"

He then decided that he would take action immediately, no matter how small, to move himself towards his dreams.

He'd remembered reading that every journey must begin with a single step. Well, his journey had now begun, he'd thought with mounting excitement. His first step into action was to get packed up and leave his home in search of a better life.

It was just beginning to get light outside, as the morning sun bid farewell to the night sky and greeted the new day. Chuck could not remember when last he'd felt so content with life, as he'd packed together his meager belongings and thought about the adventure ahead. He'd smiled happily to himself, as at last he was doing something about his dreams.

When he was all packed he had gently awoken Chip to break the news. He hadn't bothered to ask Chip to join him, as he'd known he would be wasting his words. As expected, Chip had angrily called him a fool who was chasing silly dreams like a child. He'd insisted that Chuck would soon come running back like a scared dog with his tail between his legs.

But Chuck's mind had been made up and no amount of insults or threats could keep him from reaching for his dreams. For the first time in his life Chuck felt like he had a purpose and direction.

Early on that fine summer morning, long before the rest of the world was rising to greet the new day, Chuck had already left his old life behind him, as he'd walked to the 'big city' and towards his new life. Saying goodbye to Thandi had been the most difficult part of his decision, but he'd promised her that he would return. He'd realized that just by walking away from the only life he'd ever known, he had taken the first step towards his dreams. He had at last had the courage and determination to take some decisive action to turn his dreams from mere wishes into reality. Chuck had learnt the next valuable life skill on the road to achieving your dreams in life.

Life Skill 4
Take Action!

I *have always been a man of few words. I listen more than I talk. But every now and then when something really irritates me, I become a man of many words. Now I want you to pay attention, as it is time for me to tell you about something that really aggravates me and I have much to say about it.*

I constantly meet people who whinge and whine endlessly about one thing or another. Maybe you are like these people. Let me give you some examples and see if any of them sounds familiar:

"I'm so unhappy in my relationship."

"I hate my job."

"If only I wasn't so overweight."

"I'm tired of battling and not having the good things in life."

I could write a book full of the complaints I constantly hear day in and day out from people. But can I tell you something? All this complaining gets them absolutely nowhere!

Why does it get them nowhere? Because the whingers, whiners and wishful thinkers DO NOTHING about their situation! They're often experts when it comes to moaning and groaning, but useless at doing anything about it. They're masters at offering excuses for their failures and lack of success and their true talent often lies in blaming others or outside forces for everything that goes wrong. Do any of these excuses sound familiar?

"I come from a poor family."

"I hardly have any education."

"I had a terrible upbringing."

"I've had a rotten deal in life and just seem to attract bad luck."

"I live in a terrible country with no opportunities."

If this sounds like you, be assured you're going nowhere fast! It's like anything in life, you can debate, talk, whine, moan, screech and squeal for as long as you like, but as I said, it doesn't get you anywhere. It's taking action by doing something constructive about your situation that makes things happen.

So what do I say to all the whiners, whingers and wishful thinkers? It doesn't matter what they're complaining about; whether it's their job, relationship, physical appearance or hard times, my response is always the same. "WHAT ARE YOU DOING ABOUT IT?"

This question stops them in their tracks because it's the last thing they expect or want to hear. You see, they expect you to join them in their whinging and whining, agree with them and sympathize with them. They certainly don't want to hear you ask the unthinkable, "WHAT ARE YOU DOING ABOUT IT?" This is because they usually don't plan to do anything about it. It's too much work, effort, responsibility or willpower to do anything. By asking them this question, you have now cornered them into facing the uncomfortable reality that they have no plan, intention or energy to really do anything about it.

If you believe in yourself, know what you want and have a plan to achieve it, you have to ask yourself this one important question: "What am I doing to get there?" Most of the people who have made a success of their lives are no different from you and I. What makes them different from those that never achieve much is simple: they take action to make their dreams come true.

If all we needed were dreams to succeed in life, we would all be living our ultimate lives now. Acting on our dreams is what makes them happen. Without this action, they will remain forever in our imaginations. Don't get me wrong, it's wonderful to dream, but it's only wishful thinking if you're not doing anything to make it happen.

What I mean by taking action, is that you must do something every day, no matter how small, to move you closer to your dreams. When you chip away at your plan on a daily basis, breaking each step down into smaller more attainable ones, then even what seems to be your most impossible dream will eventually become a reality. Everything is manageable, if you break it down into smaller parts and deal with each small step one at a time. Before you know it, you will have accomplished this seemingly unattainable dream.

I believe, that you can learn more about a person in only one hour of action, than in an entire year of just talking. In other words, actions always speak louder than words.

Whilst chipping away at your plan by taking action, I want you to remember this famous saying by Lao-tzu, "A journey of a thousand miles must begin with a single step." So begin your journey now as we rejoin Chuck on his journey to his dreams!

Part 5

Don't Let Negative Emotions Hold You Back!

You can never hope to discover new oceans, if you fear and worry about losing sight of the shore.

Unknown

Chapter 5

Banish Those Negative Emotions

Chuck arrived in the city excited and full of hope for the future. He was a little awestruck by the sheer size of the place and the masses of people that were bustling around. The throngs of people and the busy traffic were dwarfed by the many tall buildings and for a while Chuck just stood and stared open-mouthed at everything. He'd never been into the city before. Sure, he'd heard a lot about it, but actually being there was a different story. The noise was overwhelming and everyone seemed to be in a hurry, pushing and rushing to get somewhere. It was nothing like the peaceful, unhurried life he'd left behind.

All at once, Chuck had become very afraid. He was surrounded by strangers and was further away from home than he had ever been. Everything was so different to what he was accustomed to and he was suddenly very wary of the unknown, which had seemed so exciting to him only hours before. Fearful thoughts had crept into his mind – "What if I'm not accepted here? What if I cannot survive?" He had worried about whether he would find work and shelter. He'd worried about ending up alone and destitute. He'd still had the money that Colby had given him and he'd been determined not to waste it. His next step if he was to reach his dream of becoming a teacher was to use this money to make more money in order to finance his education.

So, he had spent his first day in the city just looking around and trying to familiarize himself with his strange new surroundings. He'd set aside some money for food, but did not want to waste money on shelter. So his first night in the city was spent sleeping under a bridge close to a busy freeway in order to escape the light drizzle.

Lying awake and listening to the constant hum of the traffic overhead, he had never felt so alone and lost before. Fear and worry had gnawed at him, making him feel almost ill with indecision. His troubled thoughts had lingered on some of his brother's last words – "You're a fool! You'll come running back like a scared dog with its tail between its legs." – Well, truth be told, he certainly had been scared and he did feel like packing up and fleeing back home. Perhaps his brother had been right, he'd thought, as he'd eventually fallen into a restless sleep.

The following day, Chuck had awoken feeling much better about everything. While he was sleeping many troubled thoughts had tumbled about confusingly in his mind, until he had eventually taken charge of them and come to a decision. The strange thing was that once he had made his decision to stop feeling scared and sorry for himself and instead focus on looking for opportunities, most of his worries and fears seemed to vanish.

That day, he had chatted to a number of people and had learnt that jobs were very scarce, with unemployment at an all time high, particularly for the uneducated. Chuck had been determined not to let this put a damper on his high spirits. He'd fought off his negative emotions by deciding to create his own opportunities. If there were no jobs, he would simply have to create one for himself.

He had watched as people sold all types of goods on the side of the road. Some of them had even ventured into the busy traffic to sell their wares, which ranged from coat hangers to rubbish packets, cold drinks, sweets and fruit. He'd watched them for a long time and saw that some of them were indeed making money. He'd then approached a few of them for advice saying that he was also interested in buying and selling as they were. They'd been less than helpful, practically chasing him away with stern threats to protect what they considered to be their "area or territory".

Chuck had noticed a toothless old lady laughing knowingly at him from across the road. When he'd approached her to find out what was so funny, she'd told him that he was wasting his time. There were far too many street traders already and her advice to him was to go back to where he'd come from. Again, doubts had threatened to overwhelm Chuck, as the uncertainty of his situation became clear.

Once more Chuck had subdued his fears and worries by taking action. He'd decided to try his hand at buying and selling regardless and had spent the rest of the day walking through the city visiting shops and pricing their goods. He'd soon come to realize that he could buy fruit and vegetables for a discount if he bought in bulk. He could then sell them for a reasonable mark-up, making a tidy profit. So he'd made a decision to make a success of buying and selling fruit and vegetables.

The following morning, Chuck had used some of his money to buy a basket and fill it with apples, bananas and peaches. He'd then found a street corner where no one seemed to mind his presence and he'd set up business.

There he'd sat for most of the day with not one person stopping to buy his fruit. Understandably, he'd become quite desperate as he'd spent most of his money on this idea. He'd bravely overcome the panic threatening to surface.

Yet again he'd fought off these negative emotions by taking action. He'd decided that if people would not come to him to buy his fruit, then he would go to them. So he'd weaved his way in and out of the busy traffic, wearing his biggest smile yet and selling his heart out. Hours later, poor Chuck had still not made one sale and he was on the verge of giving up. Just when he'd been contemplating eating all the fruit himself and going back home a defeated young man, a car packed with a family of six had stopped and purchased his entire basket full of fruit.

That night, curled up beneath a number of cardboard boxes under the shelter of the bridge, which he'd decided was to be his home for the next few days, he had felt excited and alive again. He now had more money than he'd had to begin with, which was more than he had ever had before. His plan was working.

From his position just under the bridge, he'd still had a good view of the starlit night above. The stars had become like his friends, watching over him and acting as constant reminders of the great wide world of opportunities and adventures waiting to be discovered. That night he lay back looking up at the stars and again he'd wondered what he would see if he were amongst the stars and looking back down upon himself. The picture was quite different now, he'd thought. He would see a young man who was not afraid of going after what he wants from life. A young man who had learnt that he must not let fear and worry stop him from achieving his dreams. He had worried that he wouldn't find a place to sleep, but he'd found one. True, it wasn't much, but it would do for a start. He'd worried that he wouldn't find work, but he had created a job for himself. He had worried that he wouldn't sell his wares and he'd sold everything.

Well, he'd thought, most worries and fears never actually happen. He'd learnt to overcome these negative emotions by taking action. He'd become determined never to let worry and fear stop him from achieving his dreams. On this note he'd drifted off into a peaceful and content sleep under the watchful eyes of the stars.

Yes, Chuck had indeed learnt another valuable life skill on the road to achieving his dreams.

Life Skill 5
Stamp Out Worry And Fear

*D*uring *my lifetime I have had many worries and fears. Most of them and I mean more than 99% of them never happened. Most of these negative emotions come from our imagination and not from our physical reality. If you look back over the years, you too will see that most of your worries and fears were only a figment of your imagination.*

Often these troubling thoughts are things we cannot change or are simply trivial things, which certainly don't warrant upsetting ourselves over. You have to ask yourself, "What am I worrying about? What do I fear? Is this thing really worth the stress it is giving me?" Chances are you'll probably find that it's something relatively unimportant. Don't waste your precious time and energy on always expecting the worst. It simply isn't worth it!

Have you ever seen one of those tiny Japanese Bonsai trees, which are fully grown, but remain very small? The reason for their lack of growth is because they are continuously trimmed.

When you are filled with negative emotions like worry and fear, you are like a Japanese Bonsai tree. This is because these negative emotions limit you from growing to your full potential and achieving your dreams.

As we have seen with Chuck, there is only one way to rid yourself of negative emotions. Keep busy, by taking action and facing your fears and worries. When we are busy with our mind full of the challenges of the day, it is difficult for worry and fear to settle in. It is when we are doing nothing or lying in bed with the lights out that we begin to feel those negative thoughts creeping in.

Most people who have achieved success in any area of their lives have learnt the benefit of replacing these negative emotions with action. They do not waste their time and energy on trivial worries and fears. They make firm decisions and take immediate action, avoiding lingering too long on a problem and allowing these emotions to surface.

As you and I march across the decades of time, we are going to encounter a lot of worries and fears. We are then faced with a choice. We can either deal with them and move forward or we can ruin our lives by not moving past them. You and I will endure a smoother journey if we choose not to allow these negative emotions to stop us from achieving our dreams. The choice is yours...

Part 6
Time!

Live every day as if it is your last.
One day you will be right.

Anon

Chapter 6
Time Waits For No One

Days turned into weeks and the weeks became valuable months in Chuck's life. He had learnt a lot about business during this time. He'd learnt the best roads from where to sell. He knew to increase his stock at the end of the month as people spent more after payday. He discovered where to find the cheapest quality fruit and vegetables in the city. He had also become an expert at pushing sales by encouraging people to buy from him repeatedly.

After his first month, he had progressed further by moving from under the bridge into a small room in a boarding house. Sure, it wasn't much, but he had a proper solid roof over his head and a genuine bed to sleep on – something he'd never had before. He was even able to buy himself some clothing and he was eating three good meals a day.

Chuck had also made many friends during this time. People were drawn to this energetic and enthusiastic young man with the big friendly smile and good nature. Even the other street traders who had chased and threatened him at first, had since befriended him, eager to share stories and advice with him.

After three months had passed since his arrival in the city, Chuck had already saved a considerable amount of money, which he intended to put towards furthering his education. Every day was valuable in that he learnt more about how to improve his small business and saved a little more towards his studies. His only regret was that he was unable to share his new-found success with anyone. He missed his brother Chip terribly and he longed to see Thandi, the love of his young life.

So Chuck had decided that it was time to visit his brother and friends for the weekend. He'd hoped to convince Chip to return to the city with him. He also planned to declare his love for Thandi and tell her that if she was prepared to wait for him, he would send for her when he was further established and ready to support a family.

Chuck had arrived back at his old home in the early hours of a bright Saturday morning. Chip had been overjoyed to see Chuck again and the two of them had spoken for many hours about the happenings of the past three months. Chuck had done most of the talking as nothing much, if anything had changed in Chip's life. He'd still been waking up early every morning and doing his rounds of the dumps, day in and day out. He was still wearing the same clothes, sitting around with the same people and moaning about the same things. Their humble shack was unchanged, if not even more dilapidated than when Chuck had last seen it. All in all it was as though time had stood still for Chip and his friends as everything was exactly as it had been before Chuck had left.

Once the brothers had caught up sufficiently on one another's lives, Chuck had headed off to see Thandi. The thought of her had made his heart beat fast and loud until he thought it might explode from nervous anticipation.

As it turned out, Thandi had been just as excited to see him again and the two young lovers had chatted for a long time about their future together. Chuck had shared his dreams and plans with her and she'd never once doubted him by questioning whether or not he would succeed. She'd never once laughed or mocked him and instead appeared to be proud of his achievements and impressed by his enthusiasm. Most importantly, she had eagerly agreed to wait for Chuck to come for her when the time was right.

His reunion with Thandi had gone far better than he could ever have hoped and he'd lived up to his nickname as he'd strolled happily back to his old shack, chuckling happily to himself. On his way, he was stopped by some of the elders who had gathered together in the late afternoon to enjoy a drink and a puff while sharing some stories. Chuck had always been very fond of these toothless old men with their deeply wrinkled and weather beaten faces that so easily and readily broke into smiles. He'd always loved to hear their stories and they'd always been more than eager to share them. That day it was Chuck who told them the story of his adventure thus far and they'd listened with open admiration and fascination.

To Chuck's surprise, they had almost sighed as one when he had finished, nodding their heads in unison, some looking dreamily into the distance, while others clucked unhappily to themselves. It seemed they were all deep in their own thoughts, until the silence had been broken by one of them who'd patted Chuck on the back, congratulating him for his courage to go after his dreams. The same old man had admitted that he too had had many dreams as a young man, but that he'd never even tried to accomplish them. He'd always intended doing something about them, but he'd never quite got around to it and then before he knew it here he was, an old man for whom time had almost run out. Another of the bony old men had agreed, saying that he'd always wanted to leave the settlement and see more of the world, but he'd never even been as far as the nearest city before. Another regretted that he'd never followed his dream of becoming a professional soccer player. His friends agreed that he'd always had the potential, but had never really believed in himself enough to do anything about it and so his obvious talent had been wasted.

One by one, each of these old men who Chuck had always looked up to, told their story of regret and "if only's". Some of them had a list of regrets even longer than Chuck's list of dreams. Their regrets were full of things they should have done and said. People and places they should have seen and lives they could have and should have lived. When Chuck had left there was not one of them who did not have a faraway look in his eyes, as they sat wistfully thinking of what could have been.

That evening after a hopeless attempt at trying to convince Chip to return to the city with him, Chuck had sat alone outside their shack for a long time watching the stars and thinking. It had seemed like the stars were winking and smiling back down at him. They seemed to reflect his happiness and sense of relief at escaping a wasteful life.

Sitting there, staring up at the stars he'd contemplated what he'd learnt. He'd recalled his conversation with his brother and again it occurred to him that there had been no changes in Chip's life in the past three months. Nothing had got better and if anything he seemed even worse off than before. He had not progressed and grown. Indeed, instead of going forwards, he seemed to be going backwards in life. Chuck suddenly realized that his brother and friends were wasting valuable time, which could never be retrieved. He realized, that they would one day be like the old men, full of regrets and "if only's".

It also struck Chuck that Chip always moaned about the same things, yet did nothing about them. He also blamed his past, particularly his upbringing for his present situation. "If Dad hadn't taken us out of school, I may have stood a better chance of making something of myself." "If we weren't always so poor, I'd have had more fun in life and been a happier person today." "If Mom and Dad hadn't died in that fire, things might have been a lot easier and better for us." Chuck had heard all these things from Chip many times before and it dawned on him that Chip could not let go of the past. One could not live in the past or blame the past and expect the future to take care of itself. He'd read that somewhere and now it made sense to him. Chip would never be able to progress and move forward in life until he let go of the past and started doing things today to make a better future for himself.

Chuck's thoughts had then returned to the old men. For them, it was too late to make the most of their time. Chuck was suddenly very happy and thankful that he had his whole life still ahead of him. He still had plenty of time to reach for his dreams and arrive at the end of his days with no regrets and "if only's". He aimed to make the most of every valuable second that was available to him, for if one thing was certain, it was that time waits for no man, but runs out for many.

Life Skill 6
Don't Waste Time

If you were told that you only had six months left to live, how would you spend each second of it and how different would it be from your time spent the previous day? I am certain, you would act completely different. You would certainly want to make the most of every second! What you should be doing, is living every day as though there is a time limit on your life, for you have no way of knowing when your time will run out. You do not want to leave this world wishing for so much more from life.

What really saddens me is that every day, millions of people all over the world arrive at the end of their days without reaching their dreams and making the most of their time here. Surely you don't want to become like these people who get to the end of their lives and look back only to realise how they have wasted their time. If they could have all their days over again, do you think they would now cherish and make the most of every precious second? You bet they would!

Do yourself a favour and go spend a day at an old age home talking to those who are nearing the end of their days. You are sure to find that most of them have a long list of regrets and if given the opportunity, they would do anything to go back and relive their lives. It will be a good lesson for you to make sure that you don't end up like them.

There are three major points that Chuck learnt about the importance of using his time wisely. The first thing he realized was that when he went back to his old home after three months, his brother and friends had not progressed at all. It was as though they had wasted three whole months of their lives while he had learnt and grown in so many ways. It had dawned on Chuck that his brother and friends were like many people who never reach their dreams or achieve much in life because they waste much of their lives away. They just plod on from day to day without any ambition or direction while their time here slips away.

If you ever hope to improve your life, you must honestly ask yourself "Am I making the most of every day so that I can eventually reach all my dreams? Or am I like Chuck's brother and friends who are just plodding along without any ambition or direction while my time here slips away?"

The second point that Chuck realised was to learn from his brother's inability to put the past behind him. He realised that his brother's thoughts were so caught up in the past that it left him no time to focus on the present as well as planning for the future.

I suggest that you should ask yourself the following question, "Am I worrying about the past, wishing for the past, depressing myself over the events of the past or blaming the past for my present situation?" If your answer is yes to any part of this question, then this is a large obstacle standing in the way to your dreams.When your thoughts are always on past victories, previous relationships, opportunities missed and mistakes made, you create within yourself feelings of insecurity, worry, fear and uncertainty, which adversely affect your future decisions.

Don't misunderstand me, it's normal to keep happy memories of the past alive, as long as you are intent on making more happy memories instead of hankering only after old ones.

The past can be beneficial only if we use our good memories to motivate us for the future and if we learn from our past mistakes and then put them behind us.

The past is dead and gone. It is pointless for anyone to dwell on what was or could have been. To move forward and progress in life, we have to let go of the past. It is impossible to make something worthwhile of our future if we're living in the past. We cannot do anything about the past, but we can do something about today and tomorrow.

The final point that Chuck learnt about the importance of time was not to be like many of the elders who had put things off for another day, but never got around to it. They kept telling themselves they really must do something about their situation, but they never got around to it. They never found the time in their routines to make changes for the better. Sure, they could console themselves when they were younger by saying, "It's bearable for now," but as the years had passed and nothing had changed they felt even more stuck in their unhappy situation and it was not so bearable any more.

People like these are unhappy and complain endlessly about their lives. Well, the only way to break free of a rut is through doing something about your situation. One of my heroes, Muhammad Ali explained it so well when he said, "The man who views the world at 50 the same as he did at 20 has wasted 30 years of his life."

Now one last question you must ask yourself regarding the importance of time. "Are you stuck in a rut? Perhaps you're trapped in a relationship you definitely should not be in? Maybe you wake up every morning around about the same time to get ready for the job you would rather not do? Then drive the same route to work and see the same faces every day that you would rather not see? Do you then do the same monotonous tasks every day when you would far rather be doing something else?" If your answer is yes to any part of this question then it is time you stop putting things off and start doing something to better your situation.

The overall solution to using your time wisely is quite simple. Whether you waste time, live in the past or put things off for another day, there is one solution to overcome them all. From this day on you must make a point of doing the most *important or productive thing as often as possible. Doing this one thing will ensure that you progress in life. What are you waiting for? Keep asking yourself, "What is the most productive thing I can do right now?" And DO IT!*

Think back to the last 24 hours! Was this time wasted? What about the next 24 hours? Are you going to waste them as well, or are you going to start making your time count?

So, I encourage you to live life to the full and not waste your limited time here. This will ensure that you will not end up with regrets like the old men, but rather with wonderful memories and a life full of achievement. It's your choice...

Part 7
Think About It!

Fill your mind with the right positive thoughts.
Protect your mind from the wrong negative thoughts.
Now prepare yourself for unimaginable rewards.

Warren & Sally

Chapter 7

It's The Thought That Counts!

Chuck had been rather relieved to get back to his small room in town. The weekend spent back at the settlement with his brother had opened his eyes to the waste of time and potential that had been a part of his life for so long. He was so happy that he had left his past life behind him in search of a better one. He had made a little promise to himself always to make the most of his time unlike those he had left behind.

Chuck had never let go of his dreams. Every night his thoughts and images before he drifted off to sleep were the same. He would see himself teaching, driving a nice car, living in a lovely home and going for long walks on the beach with Thandi. This is what he wanted and the desire to make it all come true urged him to continually work on improving his present situation.

As I mentioned before, Chuck had become very popular due to his friendly and happy nature. He was always positive and optimistic, choosing to see the bright side of all situations. This trait drew many people to him as they were revitalised by his positive energy, which was a refreshing change compared with the draining force of the majority of negative people.

In conversation, Chuck had mentioned to his new friends his desire to improve his situation. He'd even told them about his dream of becoming a teacher and their response was always the same. "You're crazy. You're just an uneducated street trader like us. What you want is impossible. This is as good as it gets for people like us. Why don't you just accept things as they are instead of always trying to change them?"

Chuck had realized that their responses had sounded very familiar. Were they not almost identical to the words of his brother and friends when he had spoken to them of leaving the settlement in search of a better life? Whenever he wanted to improve his situation, the people around him tried to persuade him not to change. They believed that they were stuck in their situation and unable to move up in the world.

This is when a life-changing revelation had dawned on young Chuck. He thought about when he was a garbage sifter in the shacks and everyone around him had told him that it was impossible to better himself. Well, he'd proved them all wrong. They were all still in the same situation, battling to survive from day to day while he was now successfully selling fruit and vegetables and was able to live a lot more comfortably and even save for his studies. He had managed to move up a level in life while they had remained at the bottom with only themselves to blame.

He had moved up from a lowly garbage sifter to a more respectable street trader. Now that he'd wanted to move up yet another level, the people around him were again telling him exactly the same thing. "Don't fool yourself Chuck. It's impossible to better your situation any further. Just be happy that you've got this far and make the most of your life as a street trader." Well, Chuck would not simply settle for life as a street trader.

Chuck realized that there was a definite pattern emerging. He saw that if he somehow managed to rise above his present situation as a street trader and move up to the next level, the people on that level would respond to his ideas of enhancing himself in very much the same way as the street traders before and his brother and friends before them. Why? Because people become comfortable at a certain level and because they do not believe that they can rise above their situation, they believe it's impossible for anyone else in the same situation as them to do so.

Chuck realized that no matter how much he improved himself and how many levels he moved up in life, there would always be people around him who would try to persuade him that he could not do it. These people had created a ceiling in their lives, which was preventing them from moving up another level. Chuck thought of it like someone trying to climb to the next level of a ladder so that they could see further, but being unable to move up as there was a barrier blocking the way ahead. Chuck realized that you create your own ceiling in life.

In other words, you create your own limits to how far you can grow and succeed. Chuck was stunned that more people did not see this. He decided that he would never let the negative beliefs and thoughts of other people influence him again. He decided that he was going to stay focused on his dream, no matter what and he knew that if he just stayed positive, then opportunities would come his way.

Chuck decided to keep his mind focused on what he wanted and to avoid negative people and negative thoughts wherever possible. When the people around him spoke about how bad things were and blamed everything but themselves for their situation, Chuck never fell into the trap of adding his bit of negativity. Instead, he would avoid these people unless he had something positive to add. He refused to join them in their negative whinging and whining.

As Chuck began to see the positive in every situation and his mind was so tuned into thinking only positive thoughts, he started to see opportunities everywhere. He realized that you will see what you condition yourself to see. If you are negative and never expect to see any opportunities, then you will never see any. Being so positive had opened up his mind to the possibilities out there and he saw that there were plenty. In fact, now that his mind was focused most of the day on his dreams and not on negative thoughts about failure, worry and fear, he could not believe all the opportunities around him and he was surprised that he'd never been aware of them before.

Chuck had felt like running through the streets and sharing

this new-found knowledge with his friends. But he knew that it was a pointless exercise, for until they got their minds focused on what they wanted instead of on what they couldn't have, they would never understand and never see all the opportunities he could now clearly see. He simply could not believe that he had not seen it before. It was as though his eyes had opened up fully for the first time and he was starting to realize how people became successful. It was this positive focus that made people successful! Suddenly he saw everything in a different light and it dawned on him how he could make a lot more money.

Before I go on to tell you what Chuck did to make himself a lot more money, let me first discuss with you the next important life skill that Chuck had learnt.

Life Skill 7
Choose The Right
Positive Thoughts

Pay careful attention, for what I am about to tell you is very important if you ever want to make a success of your life. If you can grasp the importance of this life skill as Chuck did, and apply it to your life, a wealth of opportunities will open up for you.

What do you think about all day long? You may not think that this is an important question, but let me assure you that what you think about all day long is of vital importance, as the thoughts going through your mind day in and day out eventually make up the person you are.

Confused? Let me explain a little further.

We think about all kinds of things all day long: We think about what happened to us yesterday and the day before; What we want to do today; Our likes and dislikes; What we want for meals; Where we want to go this weekend. We think thoughts of love, hate, fear, worry, excitement, ambition and progress. I could go on and on. Whether we like it or not, the thoughts we think about repeatedly eventually influence and mould us into the person we become.

Think about someone who is successful in all areas of their lives. What do you believe that person thinks about all day long? Well, if you could listen in on their thoughts, chances are their mind would most certainly be dominated by positive thoughts. They would probably be focused on where they are going in life, how to better themselves, success, love, sincerity, optimism, courage, ambition and confidence.

What about the thoughts of someone who has achieved nothing or very little in life? These people are often lazy, blame others for everything, waste time and do nothing about their situation. Would their mind be dominated with thoughts of success, happiness or ambition? I don't think so! Their mind would more likely be dominated by thoughts of envy, hate, jealousy, worry, fear and failure. I doubt very much they would be focused on where they are going in life.

Let me add to this by saying that if I could look in on your thoughts and see what you think about all day long, I would be able to see whether you would be a success or a failure in life.

What I am trying to say to you is this, "You simply cannot allow yourself to underestimate the importance of what you think. What you think is what you are!"

So if your mind is dominated by confident thoughts, you will become a confident person.

If your mind is dominated by weak thoughts, you will become a weak person.

If you have thoughts on self-pity you will become a person filled with self-pity. If you have loving thoughts you will become a loving person.

If you have fearful thoughts you will become a fearful person.

If you continually think about all the reasons why you will never succeed in life, you are creating a person who has all the reasons in the world not to succeed and is sure to fail.

The key to achieving what you want from life lies in your ability to dwell on the right positive thoughts. By repeating thoughts or statements, day in and day out, you eventually convince your subconscious that these thoughts or statements are true. These then become deep-rooted beliefs and your subconscious will find ways to make them a reality, even against your better judgement.

When you mentally repeat to yourself, "stupid fool," or "I can't do it," or feed your mind with words like worthless, ugly, stupid, dumb, it eventually becomes a belief in your subconscious and you will start behaving like this.

Now that you understand that success is a matter of choosing the right positive thoughts, how do you develop a mind that is dominated by positive thoughts? It is easy to say, "Think only positive thoughts and positive things will come your way," but the truth is you cannot just wake up one morning and decide to only think positive thoughts from now on. We all have our own problems, worries and fears that occupy our minds and it is not easy to simply discard these negative thoughts completely. It has to be done gradually until it becomes a habit.

Starting today, I want you to dedicate one hour of each day to thinking only positive thoughts. For just one hour a day I want you to find a quiet place where you will not be disturbed. During this time, try only to think about your dreams in life, what you have to be thankful for, what you can do today to better yourself and how you can help others. You will find that it is quite normal for negative thoughts to try and creep in even during this short time of trying to think positively. When they do, just force them aside and replace them with a positive thought. After a few days of doing this, it will become easier and easier to think only positive thoughts during this time. You will discover that hours after you have completed this exercise, you will still be feeling the positive effects it generates.

Before I move on again to Chuck's story I want you to remember this, "It is a mind dominated by positive thoughts that makes it possible for people to reach their dreams and it is a mind dominated by negative thoughts that keeps others wallowing at the bottom, never amounting to anything." So I urge you to take control of your mind by choosing the right positive thoughts.

Chuck had learnt this valuable life skill and as you will see, it changed his life, just as it can change yours...

Part 8
Help Another &
You Will Help Yourself

*One of the most difficult things to give away is kindness.
It is usually returned.*

Unknown

Chapter 8
What Goes Around Comes Around

Chuck was brimming over with excitement as he contemplated the opportunities that had now opened up for him. Life had suddenly become a challenging world of endless possibilities. He could hardly wait for the following day to explore some of these opportunities further.

Chuck had not spent the next day selling. Instead he had walked through the city and watched the street traders ply their trade. The more he saw, the more excited he had become. His idea was slowly growing in his mind. The more he thought about it and the more people he saw and spoke to, the greater became his enthusiasm and excitement.

His idea was a simple one and he wondered why none of his fellow street traders had thought of it. Perhaps they didn't think big enough or were not confident enough. Could it be that it was just too much effort or that it was too risky. Whatever the case, Chuck knew that he had to try it. It was an opportunity that he could clearly see and was determined to make the most of. So what was this simple idea?

It was this simple! All the street traders had to get their goods from somewhere. If he could supply them all with these goods, but at a cheaper price, then he was sure that they would rather buy from him. They would make a higher profit and they all liked and trusted him, so they would be happy to do business with him. He would make sure that he got the products at a good discount so that he could still mark them up and sell them for a profit to the street traders. In effect it would be as though all these people were working for him as the more they sold, the more he would sell. As long as he could keep them happy by supplying them the goods on time and at a cheaper price, then it was a win-win situation with both parties satisfied. It would mean a great deal more organization, effort and initial capital outlay for Chuck, but in the long run it would also mean a great deal more money if he could successfully control and grow the idea.

As I mentioned earlier, Chuck was extremely well liked due to his friendly and open nature. His optimism and enthusiasm were contagious and people enjoyed his presence, greeting him warmly and engaging him in conversation as often as possible. So it came as no surprise that everyone Chuck had approached about his idea, welcomed the opportunity to buy their goods from him, especially if he could supply them at a cheaper rate. Only a fool would say no to a cheaper price and a pleasant young man full of ideas and ambition.

So, armed with a long list of items ranging from coat hangers to cold drinks, fresh produce and handbags, Chuck had spent the next few days looking for all these products at cheap wholesale prices. It had certainly not been as easy as he'd thought. After two exhausting days of searching the city from its centre to the outskirts, Chuck had only found about three of the items at a cheap enough rate. Nevertheless it had been a start and he was in business. Simply finding three products to supply had encouraged him enough to keep going and to find more products to add to the list of goods he already supplied.

Soon his three items grew to five, then to ten and in a matter of only a few months of successful negotiating and trading, he had grown to such an extent that he'd been able to hire several trustworthy assistants to work with him. Their job was to pick up the goods from the wholesalers and deliver them to the street traders all over the city.

I am not going to go into great detail regarding the ins and outs of Chuck's business as this would take up far too much of my time and yours. But what I will say is that it was a simple idea, which anyone could have done if they had seen the opportunity and acted upon it as Chuck had done.

What I will also add is that much of Chuck's success with this small thriving business was due to his attitude and understanding of people. Chuck's philosophy throughout his life had been to be kind, helpful and understanding to all he met. For this reason he had easily made many friends, developing and maintaining strong relationships with everyone he came into contact with. People liked him, so they naturally preferred to do business with him rather than another and those he supplied to and bought from soon became extremely loyal to him.

You see Chuck genuinely cared about and was interested in the people around him and in turn they all cared about him. In always giving so much of himself, he became all the more popular and successful.

Although eventually he no longer had to be involved in the day to day running of the business as he had a number of trusted staff and friends to do this, he regularly visited the street traders, shopkeepers and wholesalers on whom his business relied. He chatted and laughed with them, listened to their problems with genuine concern, offered kind words and advice where necessary and always had something good to say. For all these reasons, the simple truth was that people liked to deal with him. In fact they wanted to deal with him.

Chuck may well have been unaware of this life skill, as it was not something he had learnt, but something which came naturally to him from birth. However it is a lesson that many of us need to learn if we want to achieve our dreams in life.

Life Skill 8
Be Kind, Helpful & Understanding To All You Meet

*M*ost people cannot believe that the simple act of being kind, helpful and understanding to all they meet can possibly have any major effect on their lives. But let me assure you that it is a fact that it is guaranteed to improve every aspect of your life.

By helping others you will be too busy to worry and feel sorry for yourself and therefore you will rid yourself almost entirely of depression and worry. By being friendly and understanding you will also create an abundance of happiness by attracting new friends and receiving warmth and affection from all you meet. Kindness is something that will naturally be returned to you tenfold as it attracts riches and blessings from others. Amongst other things you will also create a tremendous boost for your physical and mental well-being as you will feel good about being kind, helpful and understanding.

Remember, that often it is just the small things in life that make all the difference, like a kind word, a friendly smile, a helping hand or a word of encouragement when it is really needed. These things cost you nothing, yet the rewards may last a lifetime.

Do me a favour and try it out just for one day. You will then see for yourself the difference it makes even in such a short time. For just a day, give a friendly greeting to all those you come in contact with regardless of their position in life. Offer kindness and encouragement to those who clearly need it. Compliment, praise and thank from the heart. The list of ways to help others and put a smile on their faces is endless. Putting a smile on another's face has a way of automatically putting a smile on your own. Chuck was an expert at this!

Strangely, life has a way of returning your good deeds and sometime, somehow you will be blessed tenfold – "What goes around, comes around." So the more you give of yourself, the more you will get. Just as, "The more you share, the more you will receive."

So how does this life skill help you to live the life of your dreams? Well, it makes you more likeable and approachable, opening many doors and attracting people and opportunities to you. It's an obvious fact that people would rather deal with and help someone they like and trust like Chuck.

So far, Chuck's journey has covered eight important life skills to achieving all our dreams in life. There remains only one final life skill and without this vital lesson no one would achieve anything. In fact the absence of this life skill is what causes more people to fail in life than anything else...

Part 9
Persevere!

Our greatest glory is not in never failing, but in rising up every time we fail.

Ralph Waldo Emerson

Chapter 9

Don't Wave The Flag Of Defeat

Chuck's business had been doing extremely well. After only four months of supplying his growing number of clients on the streets with their stock, he had been able to save a large amount of money and had moved into a nice one bedroom flat in a better part of town.

Then his first major obstacle had come. It had started to rain and it was predicted that it would rain solidly with little relief for at least three weeks.

The relentless rain had meant a huge reduction in people walking the city and buying from the street traders. People were in a hurry to get indoors and no longer browsed and shopped during their lunch hours or on their way to and from work. At the same time, people in the passing cars had been reluctant to roll down their windows and let in the rain and cold to buy from the street traders. The end result was that if the street traders could not sell their wares, then they could not buy more stock from Chuck and his business would come to a grinding halt until the weather cleared.

Chuck had refused to just sit back and wait for the weather to clear before resuming business. Instead of sitting around and moaning about the rain as everyone else was doing, he would not just give up and wait it out. So he had busied himself in his apartment thinking long and hard about how he could use this obstacle of the rain to benefit him in some way. Surely there was a positive to be found in every situation if you had the perseverance to keep trying and keep looking hard enough. He had never been one for giving up and he wasn't about to give up this time either.

Due to him being so positive and focused, his sharp mind had soon come up with a solution. Again he had wondered why others had not come up with this idea sooner. It was a wonderful opportunity that had seemed ridiculously obvious under the circumstances and Chuck could already see the potential and possibilities as he had rushed out of his flat to put his idea to work.

What had this brilliant, yet simple idea been? Simply this – be flexible and adjust what you are selling to suit the circumstances. In other words, Chuck had decided that if it was going to rain solidly for at least three weeks, then the obvious solution to keep sales up was to sell things for the rain.

So Chuck had managed to obtain a variety of umbrellas in all shapes, sizes and colours at an excellent bulk price as well as a wide selection of raincoats to suit all tastes and sizes. He had even obtained various plastic covers to protect bags and briefcases from the rain. All these things he had resold to the street traders who were only too happy to be back in business, congratulating him for his brilliant idea and thanking him for helping them keep up their sales in what would have otherwise been a very bad month for them. Again everyone had been a winner, particularly Chuck who had earned even more respect amongst the people, at the same time expanding his business, not to mention his ever-increasing profit margin.

This had only been the first of many major obstacles that Chuck had come across as he reached for his dreams. He had treated all of them in much the same way, never giving up and rather viewing them as challenges that he could overcome and learn from. He had also realized that many obstacles, like the rain, held hidden opportunities if only one tried to remain positive and focused, forcing oneself to see the bright side of the situation.

As Chuck's business had grown from strength to strength, he had overcome one thing after another, refusing to give up on his dreams. He had felt that he could see his dreams becoming more and more real as he'd ticked off a few more steps on the plan he had written only several months ago. "I won't give up until I have reached all my dreams and even then I'll carry on because I will have new dreams to strive for," he'd thought determinedly to himself as he'd sat on his balcony enjoying a cup of tea under the stars.

That night the stars had seemed extra bright and once more he'd found himself wondering what he would think if he were a star looking down upon himself.

"I would think - Chuck you are a star! You have already achieved what most would have said was impossible. The stars are bright tonight for they are celebrating the success of one of their own – a superstar!" Chuck had laughed heartily at this playful thought, but in reality he knew that he had reason to be proud and to feel like a star.

He had already saved more than enough money for his studies and had long ago started to attend night classes to complete his schooling. He had also inquired about a teaching diploma, which he'd planned to pursue thereafter. Thandi was to join him next month and he had already passed his learners license and was waiting to complete his drivers license so that he could pick Thandi up in his new Golf.

Yes, he was a star for making his dreams a reality. Slowly they were drawing closer and closer. Not many people could say that they were living the life of their dreams, but through perseverance and determination, Chuck was gradually getting there. He had learnt the final and most important life skill on the road to achieving all things in life – **To develop perseverance by never giving up until you have reached your goal!**

Life Skill 9
Never Give Up!

*T*here *are so many people who want to better their lives, yet it is only a handful who actually end up doing so. This is because most people give up too easily when they come across obstacles along the way.*

If you are the type of person who gives up easily, never finishing anything you start because of distractions or obstacles along the way, you can forget about achieving most of your dreams in life. Without perseverance your dreams will always remain out of your grasp, a mere figment of your imagination. Perseverance is probably the single most important quality anyone who is interested in succeeding could ever possess. Develop this quality and it will lift you when you are down, urging you to push on until you reach your dreams.

Perseverance makes all the difference between failing and winning! Without perseverance you have lost before you have even begun. No matter how often you fall and are knocked back down over and over, you are never a failure if you keep picking yourself up to try again. The only failure is in giving up and staying down. Remember the spirit of the true champion is found in those who pick themselves up every time to try anew. When you have perseverance you will win even when the deck is stacked against you.

Perseverance should not be confused with "hard work" or "the number of hours worked". It can be more accurately defined as your total commitment and determination to follow through with your plan, even in the face of defeat and criticism. It is knowing what you want and being so determined to have it that you commit your entire efforts to getting it. It means having the willpower to fight on when others wave the flag of defeat. It is the quality that truly separates the winners from the losers.

So how do you develop perseverance? It's quite simple really.

Firstly, what you are striving for must be worth it to you! Remember that if you have enough reasons to do something, you will be far more motivated to do it. So keep your mind focused on what you want and not on short-term fixes. This means persevering until you reach your goal rather than allowing yourself to be tempted by short-term benefits.

Secondly, you must make some progress every day towards the attainment of your goal – no matter how small.

Thirdly, realize that a lack of perseverance is a bad habit, which you can stop by practicing again and again the art of persistence. In other words, learn to finish what you start. This is a major failing in most people. They never seem to be able to follow through with anything and see it through till the end. The object is to practice perseverance in your every day life and it will eventually become a habit to persist until you achieve everything you set out to do.

Finally, learn not to fear obstacles, but instead to see them as challenges that you can learn from and challenges that may even hold hidden opportunities.

Although this is the last of the nine important life skills, I am not finished yet...

The Classroom

*I*t was so quiet in the large room, you could hear a pin drop. The old man looked around him at the many eager faces looking up at him and smiled to himself. He loved this part of his life – lecturing and giving motivational presentations around the country. He was in great demand and gladly accepted these invitations whenever he was able to fit them into his busy schedule.

He could see that the story he had just told about Chuck had captivated and motivated the audience before him. It was fulfilling to know that he had perhaps played a small part in inspiring his listeners to go out and try to make a positive difference in their lives.

"Just as they say that a 'cat has nine lives' so we have nine life skills that we must learn even if it takes us nine lifetimes to do so. Learn these nine lessons, understand them well and apply them to your life and you won't need nine lives to live the life of your dreams." He said breaking the silence.

"I know without a shadow of a doubt," he continued, "that if you apply these nine life-skills that Chuck learnt to your life, you will reach your dreams, no matter how unattainable they may seem at this very moment.

"But there is one word of advice you must take heed of or you will fail," he said as they shifted onto the edge of their seats to make sure they did not miss this important piece of information. "Do not skip any of these steps. You must look at these nine life skills as signposts on the road that will lead you to your dreams. If you miss out even one of these signposts you are sure to lose your way."

A flurry of hands went up as he reached for a sip of water.

"Before I answer any questions I want to go through these nine life skills one more time," the old man said.

He pointed to a young lady in the front row and asked her, "Tell me, can you remember the first life skill?"

She smiled and replied, "You have to believe that you can do anything you truly put your mind to."

"That's correct!" The old man replied. "When you start believing in yourself, the ceiling to your potential will rise a little higher so you can see further and achieve a great deal more."

He then pointed to a tall gentleman in the back who looked like he could be an athlete and asked him what the second life skill was.

"That's easy, because I found that this was my problem," the young man replied. "You must have a clear idea of exactly

what you want from life. I realize now that I need to really think about what I want before I can do anything else." He said confidently.

"Right," the old man replied. "How can you ever hope to achieve anything if you cannot even picture it to begin with? Knowing what you want is the first step to achieving it. Remember also not to worry about how you are going to achieve it. This comes later! If you worry too much about how you are going to achieve it, you will limit yourself and will not accomplish anything.

"Who can tell me the third life skill?" He asked his young audience. Almost everyone raised their hand and he pointed to a shy young man who was now brimming with confidence. "You must develop a detailed plan that will show you how to get what you want." The eager young man blurted out.

"Right again! Remember that the best way to devise a plan is to first list all the reasons that are stopping you from achieving what you want. Next, to find solutions for these reasons. Finally you must not forget to organize your solutions in the proper sequence so that they become like signposts directing you to what you want. It is as simple as that.

"Now what is the fourth life skill?" He said pointing to a large attractive girl in the front row. "To take action," she replied. "And this is where I bomb out. I know what I want and I also know how to get it, but now for the first time I know why I never achieve much. I never take action."

"That is true for most people," replied the old man. "This is where so many fail. They believe in themselves, they know what they want, they even have a plan to get it, but they lack the action. They are like a fully laden ship sitting in the harbour with no place to go. If you believe in yourself, know what you want and have a plan to achieve it, you have to ask yourself this one important question: 'What am I doing to get there?'"

The old man took another sip of water before continuing. "When you are taking action to reach your dreams you are going to come across two obstacles that stand in your way. These are the 'twin-headed monsters,' worry and fear. So the fifth life skill is not to let the negative emotions of worry and fear stop you from achieving your dreams."

He then pointed to a young woman with long braided hair. "What is the sixth life skill that Chuck learnt?"

"This is a life skill that I will never forget," she replied. "Whenever I visit my grandfather at the nursing home, he tells me this lesson, but until now I have never really understood what he was trying to get through to me. I have realized that I must use my time wisely and live every day as though there is a time limit on my life, for I have no way of knowing when my time will run out. I've also decided that I do not want to get to the end of my years wishing for so much more from life as my grandfather does." She said emotionally.

"The next life skill is to take control of what you think by choosing the right positive thoughts." A young man blurted out from the back.

"Yes," the old man replied smiling at the young man's enthusiasm. "It is a mind dominated by positive thoughts that makes it possible for men to reach their dreams and it is a mind dominated by negative thoughts that keeps others wallowing at the bottom, never rising and amounting to anything.

"Now, before we discuss the next life skill, let me say that this one is the easiest to do, yet can have the most amazing effect on all areas of your life. What is it?" He asked a big burly fellow whose chair was creaking noisily under the strain of his weight.

"To be kind, helpful and understanding to all you meet," growled the big guy shyly.

"Yes, this simple act of being kind, helpful and understanding to all you meet, will have a major effect on your life. It will make you more friends and create more opportunities for you than you could ever imagine," he continued.

"Who will tell me what the final life skill was that Chuck learnt and what we should all learn if we want to achieve our dreams?" He asked a bright-eyed student in the back.

"You must never give up." Answered the student.
"Indeed, perseverance is probably the single most important quality anyone who is interested in succeeding could ever possess. When you develop this quality, it will carry you when you are down, lifting you and encouraging you to push on until you reach your dreams."

Chuck and Thandi

*T*he old man surveyed the room full of young, eager faces and as always he felt rejuvenated by their youthful energy and vitality. He felt privileged to be able to help grow and develop young healthy minds and smiled at the class before him. It never ceased to please him when he was faced with so much promise and potential. They were the future and he knew that any and indeed every one of them had the potential to become whatever he or she wanted to and go on to achieve great things.

At this point a student seated towards the back of the classroom raised his hand enthusiastically. Like the rest of the class he'd listened attentively, engrossed in the rags to riches story. His attention span was usually very short but this special guest-speaking lecturer was proving to be quite fascinating.

"Sir, I was wondering, do you actually know Chuck? I mean, does he really exist?"

"Oh, yes my boy. I assure you, he does exist. In fact, I'd like to think we know each other quite well," smiled the old man.

Just then there was a knock at the door and an elderly woman stepped into the room. Although her greying hair was a sign of her age, her face was still full with only deep smile lines to show for her years. The well-dressed woman smiled happily at the old man, regarding him playfully and shaking her head in wonder. "Are you still here old man? It seems impossible to drag you away lately. Surely, these young ones have had enough of an old man's ramblings," she teased, eyeing him mischievously.

The young students would have to be blind not to see the love that flowed so openly and freely between these two elderly people. It shone in their eyes as they looked at one another and the students watched in amusement as the old man's face seemed to melt into an impossibly wide smile, his eyes joining in the fun as they twinkled with joy at the sight of her.

"This is my lovely wife whom I promised a lunch date, for which I am now running hopelessly late. You must always remember to make time for the important things in life. Food and love are unquestionably two of the most important things and now I must bid you farewell, so that I can attend to both. I thank the stars that my Thandi is such a patient woman," he added boyishly, winking at the blushing woman in the doorway.

A hush fell on the room. Had they just heard him say

Thandi, his wife? The students exchanged knowing looks as the possibility suddenly dawned on them. All at once many hands were thrust into the air waving frantically for attention, all of the students no doubt itching to ask the same question.

"Sir, are you Chuck?" Blurted out a dimple-faced young girl who was simply unable to contain her curiosity any longer.

The entire class leaned forward in their seats and again the silence was almost deafening in its completeness.

"No one has called him that in a long time," came the reply from Thandi still standing in the doorway. "But it does suit him, don't you think?" She said smiling back at her husband who was now grinning sheepishly like a boy who had been caught with his hand stuck in the cookie jar.

The students looked at the man before them with renewed interest and awe. He was Chuck! There were so many unanswered questions burning to be asked, so much more that they wanted to learn from this amazing man.

Chuck quietly regarded the expectant and upturned faces before him. "Tonight, I want you to look out at the stars and ask yourself, 'If I were a star out there looking back down upon myself and my life, what would I see?'

"You see, I believe we are all born as stars, but some of us lose our sparkle along the way while others live to outshine even the brightest among us. It's up to you to make your star shine and sparkle, but know this – 'there is a star somewhere within you, whether you believe it or not!' It is never too late to

discover the star within yourself and make it shine with happiness and achievement.

"My star shines a little brighter every day as I keep learning and keep striving to reach ever higher and further, thereby removing any ceiling that could cast a shadow over my star. I have no ceiling for I have made it so. There are no limits to my potential as I have removed the ceiling that hampers my progress.

"Where has my ceiling gone? Well, it was never really there. It was an invisible ceiling, self-created by my own limiting beliefs and the limiting beliefs of those around me. Raise your ceiling in life or get rid of it altogether so that your star too may shine forever brightly."

With that, Chuck picked up his briefcase and began to walk towards the door. There was a scraping of chairs and a shuffling of feet as the entire room full of students came to a stand. They all began to clap loudly for the old man as he reached his wife and held her hand. Together, Thandi and Chuck turned and looked back at the class once more and all the students in the front could clearly see the tears shining in the old man's eyes as he smiled and bade them farewell.

More Titles from the same Authors

Unleash Your Full Potential
Warren Veenman & Sally Eichhorst

This popular bestseller has been reprinted several times and is in constant demand. Its popularity stems partly from being so easy to read and to understand. It is filled with simple and practical programs, principles and philosophies, which are easy to follow and show you how to achieve and live your dreams.

The purpose of this book is to help you unleash your full potential and create the life of your dreams, whether this means more money, fame, power, love, or happiness. By the time you finish this book, you will have the knowledge and skill to succeed, irrespective of your age, physical status, background, financial situation, or education.

People from all walks of life insist that reading this book was one of the best decisions they ever made. It helped them succeed beyond their wildest expectations, just as it can help you.

Dare To Succeed
Warren Veenman & Sally Eichhorst

This thoroughly entertaining and thought inspiring book acts as a reminder that there is absolutely nothing stopping you from succeeding in life, but yourself.

The main aim of this book is to show you how you can succeed by working on the following five important areas.

- Awaken the Power Within (Positive thinking)
- Attitude and Understanding determines success
- Conquer the "Big 3" (Fear, Worry, Depression)
- Make the most of your Time
- Dare to reach your Dreams (Goals)

We assure you, when you reach the last pages, you will have all the tools necessary to succeed in life.

If I can You Can
Sally Eichhorst

Anyone can achieve their dreams, no matter what their present circumstances. We've all seen people with the odds stacked against them succeed, so why not you?

You are in control of your life and you can decide right now to make the most of it. It's never too late to really live. It's up to you to give life your all and build a life worth living. That's what this book is all about. It aims to show you how to make the most of your life by living it to the full and achieving your dreams.

This book is a challenge to be all that you can be. Not only does it make you really think about your life and the changes you may need to make, but it also shows you how to go about making these changes and creating the life of your dreams. By mastering the simple, yet detailed 6-part work theory covered in this book, you can make your journey through life an adventurous one, full of achievement and happiness.

The remarkably moving stories and powerful insights within these pages will certainly help to make your journey through life a little less difficult and a lot more meaningful. It is sure to be exciting and inspiring reading as well as an excellent practical hand-guide to achieving success and happiness in your life.

Get Your Act Together
Sally Eichhorst

This attention-grabbing book simply demands a reaction from the reader. The book contains 11 harsh but bold statements meant to kick-start you into getting your act together. The stark and brutal truth will shock some readers and rightly so, as the aim is to rattle the reader's cage into taking some positive action.

A Pocket Full Of Inspiration
Warren Veenman & Sally Eichhorst

This delightfully entertaining and talked-about little book is a power pack of inspiration and gives new meaning to the phrase "Dynamite comes in small packages."

The book is filled with amazing and thought inspiring true-life stories, which are sure to have an impact on you. The overall aim of this little gem is to lift your spirits and motivate you to greater heights. It is sure to be a moving and heart-warming reading experience, which will definitely be worth your while.

This is an excellent gift for anyone, whether for you, that special someone in your life, friends, family, clients or staff.

A Little Burst of Inspiration
Warren Veenman & Sally Eichhorst

This little gift book is an ideal keepsake filled with wonderfully entertaining and inspiring stories to warm the heart and exercise the mind. It simply bursts with inspiration!

All these books are available at your local bookshop, or can be ordered direct from the publisher.

Reach Publishers

Self-publishers and Distributors of all books

...inspire the world
with words.

P.O. Box 1384
Wandsbeck
3631
South Africa

.

Made in United States
North Haven, CT
29 March 2022